BRANCH LINES
TO
TORRINGTON

Vic Mitchell and Keith Smith

MP Middleton Press

Cover picture: The Southern Counties Touring Society railtour stands at Torrington on 3rd October 1965. The other half of the "Exeter Flyer" from Waterloo had gone to Ilfracombe. No. 80039 is one of British Railways class 4 2-6-4Ts, a type introduced in South Devon in May 1962 but seldom used in North Devon. (S.C.Nash)

Published August 1994
First reprint January 2005
Second reprint March 2013

ISBN 978 1 873793 37 4

Design Deborah Esher
Typesetting Barbara Mitchell

Published by
       Middleton Press
       Easebourne Lane
       Midhurst
       West Sussex
       GU29 9AZ
Tel: 01730 813169
Fax: 01730 812601
Email: info@middletonpress.co.uk
www.middletonpress.co.uk

Printed in the United Kingdom by IJ Graphics, Guildford, Surrey. GU2 9XW

CONTENTS

INDEX

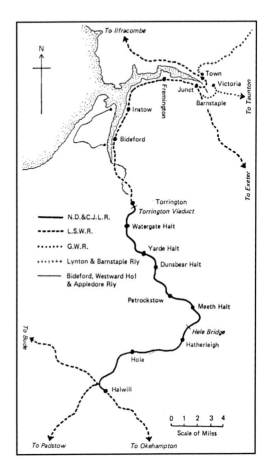

ACKNOWLEDGEMENTS

In addition to those mentioned in the credits, we would like to express our appreciation of the help received from the Bideford & Instow Railway Group, G.Croughton, Mrs. M.Field, Mrs. S.Grove, M.King, J.R.W.Kirkby, N.Langridge, Mr. D.& Dr. S.Salter, G.T.V.Stacey, N.Stanyon, Miss M.Wheeler, A.Wilkinson, E.Youldon and our ever helpful wives.

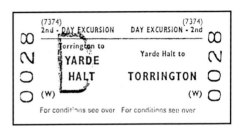

GEOGRAPHICAL SETTING

The route runs down the estuary of the River Taw for nearly six miles and then proceeds up the estuary of the River Torridge. It follows that waterway closely to Torrington. Further climbing takes the line to 450ft above sea level in the vicinity of Yarde Halt. There follows a descent which returns the track to the Torridge Valley near Hatherleigh, dropping over 250ft in altitude. Rising gradients on the final section took trains to about 600ft at Halwill.

The geology of the district is basically Culm Measures (sandstone with siltstone and shales) but in the Meeth-Petrockstow district there is an area of Bovey Clay of economic importance for pottery production and brick making.

The maps are to the scale of 25ins to 1 mile, unless otherwise stated, but there were no such maps published south of Torrington during the life of that part of the line.

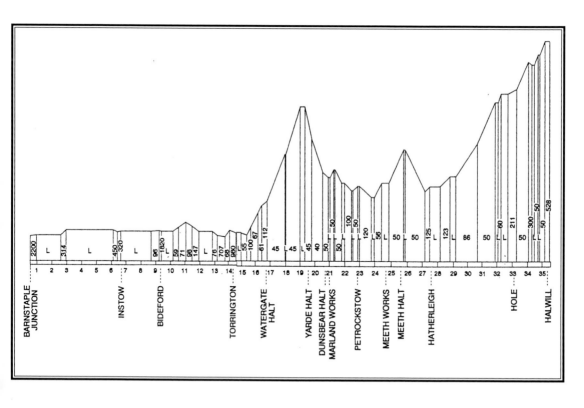

HISTORICAL BACKGROUND

While coastal trading ships were able to reach Bideford, few could sail direct to Barnstaple, the cargo being transferred at Appledore onto barges for conveyance to the town. As an alternative to this, the Taw Vale Railway & Dock Company obtained an Act on 11th June 1838 to build a dock at Fremington and a standard gauge horse-worked railway from there to the south end of the bridge over the River Taw at Barnstaple. These came into use on 25th April 1848, consent having been obtained in 1845 to extend the line to Exeter. An independent Exeter & Crediton Railway was authorised in the same year but traffic did not commence until 1851. It was built to the broad gauge and operated by the Bristol & Exeter Railway for about one year. The line was then leased to and operated by the contractor, Thomas Brassey.

The TVR's Barnstaple - Fremington line was converted to broad gauge, as its Crediton to Barnstaple section was built to that gauge. Passenger services on both parts commenced on 1st August 1854 and were extended to Bideford on 2nd November 1855.

The London & South Western Railway had shares in the TVR but was not able to lease the line until 1862, when it also leased the E&CR. The combined lines became known as the North Devon Railway and, following the addition of a third rail, LSWR standard gauge trains began running to Bideford on 2nd March 1863. Goods trains continued to use the wider track until April 1877, as did some local passenger trains which the LSWR worked with ex-contractor's stock.

The standard gauge Bideford-Torrington section was opened on 18th July 1872, the LSWR having obtained an Act for its construction on 19th June 1865. The branch from Barnstaple to Ilfracombe came into use on 30th July 1874.

The Okehampton-Holsworthy route was opened on 20th January 1879. The next development in the district was the opening of a private 3ft gauge mineral railway between Torrington and Marland on 1st January 1881. It had no Act of Parliament and was generally known as the Torrington & Marland Railway.

The North Devon & Cornwall Junction Light Railway obtained an Order under the Light Railways Act in 1914 to construct a standard gauge line from Torrington to Halwill on the Okehampton - Holsworthy route, using much of the trackbed of the TMR. Delayed by World War I, work commenced in 1922 with Col. H.F.Stephens as engineer. The NDCJLR opened fully on 27th July 1925 and was operated by the Southern Railway, although technically an independent company until 1948. The SR had incorporated the LSWR in 1923.

The SR decided that, from 1st July 1925, Torrington would be at the end of two branch lines and that Ilfracombe would cease to be on a branch, becoming the end of their main line instead.

The lines became part of the Southern Region of British Railways upon nationalisation in 1948, except for some commercial aspects for which the Western Region was responsible until 1958. That region took total control on 1st January 1963 and through working from Waterloo ceased on 5th September 1964.

Passenger services between Torrington and Halwill were withdrawn on 1st March 1965 and total closure also took place south of Meeth on that day.

Barnstaple-Torrington passenger trains continued until 2nd October 1965 and trains for clay ran until 13th September 1982, the line also being used for bulk milk traffic until 12th October 1978. The final special train ran to Torrington on 27th January 1983.

A preservation society was formed which obtained a moratorium on the track between Barnstaple and Bideford but raised insufficient funds to purchase it. The trackbed passed to Devon County Council, who eventually created a footpath and cycleway between Barnstaple and Petrockstow, now known as the "Tarka Trail".

PASSENGER SERVICES

Barnstaple - Torrington

The initial service to Bideford comprised five return journeys on weekdays with an early morning train each way on Sundays. This had increased to seven and two by 1869.

The table below gives the frequency of down trains on the route but excludes trains running less than four days per week and the short workings that were run as far as Bideford in the early years.

	Weekdays	Sundays
1872	6	1
1890	9	2
1906	11	2
1914	11	3
1924	11	4
1934	14	7
1944	10	5
1954	12	6
1965	10	5

There were many through trains from Exeter until 1925 but thereafter Barnstaple Junction was the main originating point. With the introduction of diesel multiple units on 6th September 1964, there were some through workings from Taunton and from Salisbury.

Through coaches from Waterloo were a feature of timetables for many decades. Prior to World War I, the 11.10am from Waterloo carried a luncheon car through to Torrington, arriving at 4.8pm. In the summer of 1954, there were through coaches from Waterloo at 9.0am, 11.0am, 1.0pm and 3.0pm Mondays to Fridays, with two extra on Saturdays. The overnight newspaper train also carried a through coach. Through working from Waterloo declined in the early 1960s and ceased in September 1964, with the demise of the "Atlantic Coast Express" (The ACE).

Special trains

After the withdrawal of regular services, an unusually large number of special trains were operated. Most of these are shown in the following table.

Date	From	To	Name
27. 3.65	Exeter	Circular tour	Exmoor Ranger
12. 9.65	Waterloo	Torrington	Exeter Flyer
3.10.65	Waterloo	Torrington	Exeter Flyer
10. 1.68	Bideford	Torrington	Emergency service (a)
3.10.70	Exeter	Ilfracombe	Exmoor Belle (d)
4. 6.77	Bideford	Paddington	N.Devon Jubilee
22.10.77	Bideford	Paddington	
26.11.77	Bideford	Fratton	(Football Special)
16. 7.78	Bideford	Kingswear	Heart of Devon Railtour
10. 9.78	Bideford	Kingswear	
29. 4.79	Torrington	Tour (d)	May Fair Special
27. 5.79	Torrington	York	
12. 7.79	Torrington	Paignton	S.Devon Seaside
22. 7.79	Torrington	Calstock	Tamar Cruise
5. 8.79	Torrington	Calstock	Tamar Cruise
16. 8.79	Barnstaple	Meeth	Devon Explorer II
16. 8.79	Paignton	Bideford	Devon Explorer I
2. 9.79	Torrington	Kingswear	Heart of Devon
20.10.79	Crewe	Meeth	ACE
3.11.79	Torrington	Waterloo	ACE
22. 6.80	Torrington	Calstock	Tamar Cruise
20. 7.80	Torrington	Paignton	Seaside Special
27. 7.80	Bideford	Tour (d)	
10. 8.80	Bideford	Tour (d)	
24. 8.80	Torrington	Portsmouth	Solent Tour
25.10.80	Torrington	Waterloo	ACE
9. 8.81	Plymouth	Meeth	N.Devon Explorer
25. 7.82	Barnstaple	Meeth	(Two trips)
12. 9.82	Bristol	Bideford	N.Devon Explorer (b)
16.10.82	London	Torrington	ACE
6.11.82	Bristol	Torrington	Last ACE
27. 1.83	Barnstaple	Torrington	Single railcar (c)

a) Operated free and hourly 7.30 to 18.30 most days to 19th January, due to flood damage to Bideford Bridge. Bus connection was provided from Torrington to Bideford. As the line to Exeter was closed by floods, the service was operated with the only suitable stock standing at Barnstaple. This was class 2 diesel no. D6336, a newspaper van and a DMU driving trailer. A single railcar was sent from Exeter on 13th January, when that line reopened. Clay traffic to Fremington was moved in the evenings.

b) Ran to Meldon Quarry twice.

c) Private fact-finding journey by local officials.

d) Return journeys to Meeth and Barnstaple.

LONDON (Waterloo) AND BARNSTAPLE, ILFRACOMBE AND BIDEFORD.

DOWN TRAINS.		WEEK-DAYS.					SUNDAYS.				
		a.m.	a.m.	a.m.	p.m.		p.m.	a.m.	p.m.		
WATERLOO ... dep.		1 25	9 0	10 50	12 50	...	2 50	11 0	4 0	...	...	...
Woking ... ... ,,		...	9u35	...	1u22	...	...	11u35	4u32	...	...	...
Barnstaple Junc. ... arr.		7 4	3 4	3 44	6 28	...	8 15	4 33	9 59	...	...	...
Barnstaple Town ... ,,		7 18	3 13	3 54	6 36	...	8 28	4 44	10 8	...	...	...
ILFRACOMBE ... ,,		8 0	3 52	4 36	7 16	...	9 8	5 26	10 48	...	...	...
BIDEFORD ... ... ,,		7 53	3 33	4 18	6 58	...	8 48	5 8	10 28	...	...	...

u —Take up only.

October 1944 London through trains

Torrington - Halwill

The timetables for the years of frequency are illustrated. It is noteworthy that from 1932 to 1964 there were two through trains and one or two short workings throughout the 32 year period. Only their timings changed.

1925

HALWILL, HATHERLEIGH, and TORRINGTON.—Southern.

Miles	Week Days only.	mrn	aft	aft
	Halwill ... dep.	1046	4 55	7 35
2¾	Hole	1055	5 4	7 44
7¾	Hatherleigh	1113	5 22	8 2
9¾	Meeth Halt	1124	5 33	8 13
12¼	Petrockstowe	1134	5 43	8 23
14¾	Dunsbear Halt	1144	5 53	8 33
20¼	Torrington 167 ... arr.	1210	6 22	8 59

Miles	Week Days only.	mrn	aft	aft
	Torrington ... dep.	9 0	3 5	5 25
5¾	Dunsbear Halt	9 24	3 29	5 49
8	Petrockstowe	9 34	3 39	5 59
10¾	Meeth Halt	9 46	3 51	6 11
12¾	Hatherleigh	9 56	4 1	6 21
17¾	Hole	1016	4 21	6 41
20¼	Halwill B 168 ... arr.	1026	4 31	6 51

NOTES.

B Station for Beaworthy

1926

HALWILL, HATHERLEIGH, and TORRINGTON.

Miles	Week Days only.	mrn	mrn	aft	aft	aft	aft
	Halwill ... dep.	..	1046	S	E	5 10	7 35
2¾	Hole	..	1055	..	..	5 19	7 44
7¾	Hatherleigh	..	1113	..	..	5 37	8 2
9¾	Meeth Halt	..	1124	..	..	5 48	8 13
12¼	Petrockstow	8 5	1134	..	4 36	5 58	8 23
14¾	Dunsbear Halt	8 14	1144	1 17	4 58	6 9	8 33
—	Yarde Halt	8 20	1150	1 24	5 5	6 15	8 39
20¼	Torrington 177 ... arr.	8 40	1210	1 44	5 25	6 35	8 59

Miles	Week Days only.	mrn	mrn	aft	aft
	Torrington ... dep.	6 25	9 0	3 5	5 25
	Yarde Halt	6 43	9 19	3 24	5 44
5¾	Dunsbear Halt	6 48	9 24	3 29	5 49
8	Petrockstow	7 11	9 34	3 39	5 59
10¾	Meeth Halt	..	9 45	3 51	6 11
12¾	Hatherleigh	..	9 55	4 1	6 21
17¾	Hole	..	1015	4 21	6 41
20¼	Halwill B (above) ... arr.	..	1025	4 31	6 51

B Station for Beaworthy. E Except Saturdays. S Saturdays only.

1929

HALWILL, HATHERLEIGH, and TORRINGTON.

Miles	Week Days only.	mrn	mrn	mrn	aft	aft	aft	aft	aft
	Halwill ... dep.	..	8 46	1046	S	E	4 46	6 46	8 26
2¾	Hole	..	8 55	1055	..	..	4 55	6 55	8 35
7¾	Hatherleigh	..	9 13	1113	..	..	5 13	7 13	8 53
9¾	Meeth Halt	..	9 24	1124	..	..	5 30	7 30	9 4
12¼	Petrockstow	8 8	9 34	1134	1 5	..	5 40	7 40	9 14
14¾	Dunsbear Halt	8 17	9 47	1144	1 14	5 9	5 50	7 50	9 24
16	Yarde Halt	8 23	9 53	1150	1 21	5 15	5 56	7 55	9 30
18¾	Watergate Halt	8 37	10 7	12 4	1 35	5 29	6 10	8 10	9 44
20½	Torrington 177 ... arr.	8 45	1015	1212	1 43	5 37	6 18	8 18	9 52

Miles	Week Days only.	mrn	mrn	aft	aft	aft
	Torrington ... dep.	6 25	9 0	2 27	4 22	6 22
1¾	Watergate Halt	6 32	9 7	2 34	4 29	6 29
4½	Yarde Halt	6 46	9 21	2 48	4 43	6 43
5¾	Dunsbear Halt	6 52	9 26	2 53	4 48	6 48
8	Petrockstow	7 4	9 36	3 3	4 58	6 58
10¾	Meeth Halt	7 16	9 46	3 13	5 8	7 5
12¾	Hatherleigh	7 26	9 56	3 23	5 18	7 18
17¾	Hole	7 44	1016	3 43	5 38	7 38
20½	Halwill C 179 and above arr.	7 56	1026	3 53	5 48	7 48

NOTES.

C Station for Beaworthy.

E Except Saturdays.

S Saturdays only.

1931

HALWILL, HATHERLEIGH, and TORRINGTON.

Miles	Week Days only.	mrn	mrn	mrn	aft	aft	aft	aft	aft
	Halwill ... dep.	..	8 46	1046	S	E	4 46	6 46	8 26
2¾	Hole	..	8 55	1055	..	..	4 55	6 55	8 35
7¾	Hatherleigh	..	9 13	1113	..	..	5 13	7 13	8 53
9¾	Meeth Halt	..	9 24	1124	..	..	5 30	7 30	9 4
12¼	Petrockstow	8 8	9 34	1134	1 5	..	5 40	7 40	9 14
14¾	Dunsbear Halt	8 17	9 47	1144	1 14	5 9	5 50	7 50	9 24
16	Yarde Halt	8 23	9 53	1150	1 21	5 15	5 56	7 56	9 30
18¾	Watergate Halt	8 37	10 7	12 4	1 35	5 29	6 10	8 10	9 44
20½	Torrington 177 ... arr.	8 45	1015	1212	1 43	5 37	6 18	8 18	9 52

Miles	Week Days only.	mrn	mrn	aft	aft	aft
	Torrington ... dep.	6 25	9 0	2 27	4 22	6 22
1¾	Watergate Halt	6 32	9 7	2 34	4 29	6 29
4½	Yarde Halt	6 46	9 21	2 48	4 43	6 43
5¾	Dunsbear Halt	6 52	9 26	2 53	4 48	6 48
8	Petrockstow	7 4	9 36	3 3	4 58	6 58
10¾	Meeth Halt	7 16	9 46	3 13	5 8	7 8
12¾	Hatherleigh	7 26	9 56	3 23	5 18	7 18
17¾	Hole	7 46	1016	3 43	5 38	7 38
20½	Halwill C 179 & above arr.	7 56	1026	3 53	5 48	7 48

NOTES.

C Station for Beaworthy.

E Except Saturdays.

S Saturdays only.

1932

HALWILL, HATHERLEIGH, and TORRINGTON.

Miles	Week Days only.	mrn	mrn	aft	aft	aft
	Halwill ... dep.	..	1046	S	E	6 46
2¾	Hole	..	1055	..	..	6 55
7¾	Hatherleigh	7F43	1113	..	..	7 13
9¾	Meeth Halt	7F52	1124	..	..	7 24
12¼	Petrockstow	8 8	1134	1 5	..	7 34
14¾	Dunsbear Halt	8 17	1144	1 14	5 9	7 41
16	Yarde Halt	8 23	1150	1 21	5 15	7 50
18¾	Watergate Halt	8 37	12 4	1 35	5 29	8 4
20½	Torrington 177 ... arr.	8 45	1212	1 43	5 37	8 12

Miles	Week Days only.	mrn	mrn	aft
	Torrington ... dep.	6 25	9 0	4 22
1¾	Watergate Halt	6 32	9 7	4 29
4½	Yarde Halt	6 46	9 21	4 43
5¾	Dunsbear Halt	6 52	9 26	4 48
8	Petrockstow	7 4	9 36	4 58
10¾	Meeth Halt	7F23	9 46	5 8
12¾	Hatherleigh	7F33	9 56	5 18
17¾	Hole	..	1016	5 38
20½	Halwill G 179 & above arr.	..	1026	5 48

E Except Saturdays. F Tues. only. G Station for Beaworthy. S Saturdays only.

1965

Weekdays

Halwill to Torrington

			A	A
HALWILL	d	..	10 35	18 20
HOLE	d	..	10 44	18 30
HATHERLEIGH	d	..	11 00	18 46
MEETH HALT	d	..	11 08	18 54
PETROCKSTOW	d	7 55	11 17	19 04
DUNSBEAR HALT	d	8 04	11 25	19 12
YARDE HALT	d	8 10	11 30	19 17
WATERGATE HALT	d	8 24	11 42	19 29
TORRINGTON	a	8 32	11 49	19 36

Torrington to Halwill

TORRINGTON	d	6 25	8 55	15 55
WATERGATE HALT	d	6 32	9 02	16 02
YARDE HALT	d	6 47	9 16	16 15
DUNSBEAR HALT	d	6a52	9 20	16 19
PETROCKSTOW	d	..	9 30	16 29
MEETH HALT	d	..	9 40	16 39
HATHERLEIGH	d	..	9 48	16 49
HOLE	d	..	10 08	17 08
HALWILL	a	..	10 18	17 18

A Through train to Barnstaple Junction

The timetable for the final months was unusual in showing through trains beyond Torrington, these being worked by DMUs.

1. Barnstaple to Torrington

BARNSTAPLE JUNCTION

1.   Coaches of unfamiliar proportions stand at the up platform, these being of broad gauge and probably in the ownership of Thomas Brassey, the contractor for the construction of the line. The locomotive is likely to be one of the seven 2-2-2s used on the route. There is no doubt about the power provided for shunting or that a bell was provided to indicate imminent departure of trains. (British Rail)

2.   With the River Taw in the background, class EIR no. 2094 approaches the station on 18th August 1935 with a train from Torrington. Behind the rear coach are the buffer stops of the headshunt for the siding to an industrial area, the gate being visible above the leading coach. (H.F.Wheeller)

The 1938 map at 6ins to 1 mile has the SR line from Exeter at the lower right border and the GWR route from Taunton on the right. At the top is Barnstaple Town station and the line to Ilfracombe. The route that we are to follow to Torrington is on the left.

← 3. A few minutes later, the same locomotive was recorded taking water prior to receiving coal from the wicker baskets lined up on the stage on the right. This picture was taken from the London end of the up platform. (H.F.Wheeller)

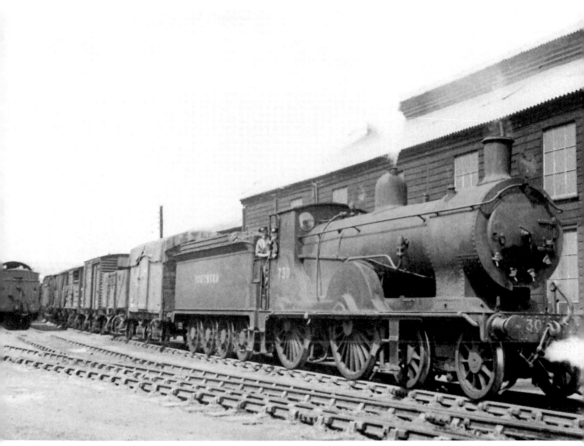

← 4. Another 1935 photograph shows class M7 no. 34 and class E1R no. 2124 standing out of steam, north of the engine shed. The machine shop is on the left and the goods shed is on the right. (H.C.Casserley)

5.   West of the engine shed on 29th June 1949 is class T9 no. 730 which is coupled to a van with a defective roof. Its train also includes cattle wagons, the cattle dock and pens being on the left of the picture. (S.C.Nash)

6.   Wagons stand on the private siding which was in use until 1967. The headshunt had been extended 242 yds in April 1945 to cope with wartime traffic. Many wooden components of aircraft were produced here. Class M7 no. 30247 is signalled for the platform road in about 1950; the ringed arm is for the through line. (C.R.L.Coles)

7.   At least three types of cattle wagon are included in this special from Torrington on 16th June 1950, which is hauled by N class no. 31875. This fine photograph could be titled "Meat and two veg", in view of the railwaymen's crop in the foreground. (J.J.Smith)

8.　　　Heavy lifting gear was provided to enable major running repairs to be undertaken. No. 32696 was rebuilt from class E1 0-6-0T to E1R 0-6-2T in 1928, having been built by the LBSCR in 1876 as no. 104 *Brittany*. Ten engines were so treated for further life in the West Country. The shed closed on 6th September 1964 but signing-on continued until 1971. (Lens of Sutton)

9.   A local service from Torrington terminates in the up platform on 29th June 1960. The locomotives are class M7 0-4-4T no. 30247 and BR class 2 2-6-2T no. 41313. The latter was probably working back to the depot after a day's labour between Torrington and Halwill.   (N.L.Browne)

10.   The station was named "Barnstaple Junction" from 1874 until 1971, when the Ilfracombe line closed. Class 700 no. 30317 was photographed on 26th June 1960 with a Maunsell composite coach and the engineers inspection coach no. DS1, the train having arrived from Torrington. (N.L.Browne)

11.   Milk from Torrington precedes the passengers as class 2 no. 41283 crosses the down Ilfracombe lines on 15th July 1963. The signal box was designated "West" until 1949 and "B" thereafter. It was in use from 1924 until 21st May 1971. The dock on the right was built on the site of three sidings that radiated from a turntable. (E.W.Fry)

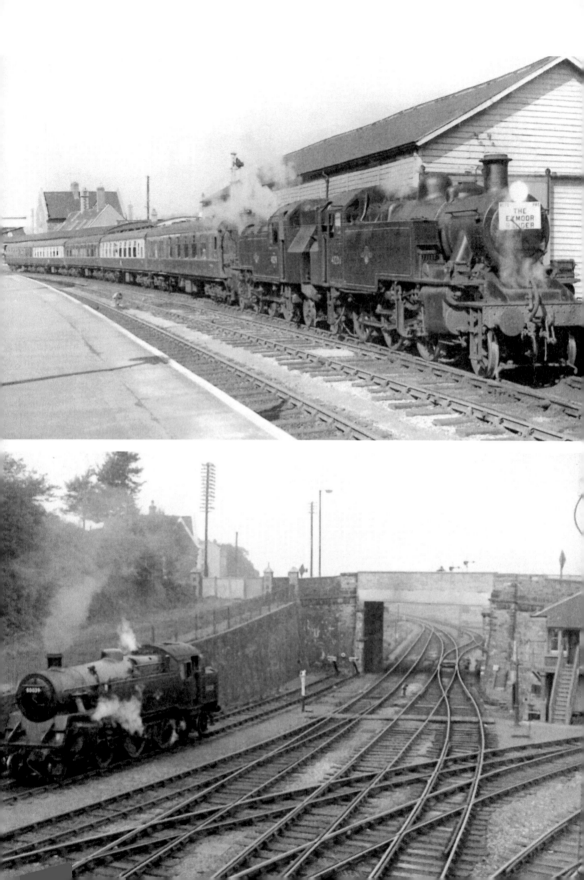

← 12. The "Exmoor Ranger" railtour on 27th March 1965 was the last train to run between Halwill and Torrington and was hauled by nos. 41306 and 41291. The tour started at Exeter and ran via Okehampton. It did a return trip to Barnstaple Victoria goods depot and then continued to Ilfracombe and back, with the help of ex-GWR 0-6-0 no. 3205. The return to Exeter was behind this engine via Taunton. (S.C.Nash)

Other views and maps of former SR stations at Barnstaple can be found in the companion albums *Exeter to Barnstaple, Branch Line to Lynton* and *Branch Line to Ilfracombe.*

← 13. The foot crossing was used by the signalman to reach the white post on which was mounted the key token carrier for the single line to Fremington. Class 4 2-6-4T no. 80039 was waiting to go on to the Torrington portion of the SCTS "Exeter Flyer" after the departure of the Ilfracombe coaches. This railtour ran on 3rd October 1965 and duplicated one run on 12th September of that year. It was advertised as the last steam in North Devon. The next time steam haulage was seen at this station was on 1st May 1994, when two locomotives of the same class arrived on opposite ends of a special train from Exeter. (D.Cullum coll.)

14. A DMU stands beyond platform 3 (which came into use in 1924) while the driver collects the single line token. Platform 2 had been added in 1874. Type 2 diesel no. D6339 approaches platform 1 with loaded clay wagons on 30th July 1969. (D.J.Aston)

← 15. A class 25 diesel waits with empty clay wagons in 1977, by which time the 1878 footbridge had been demolished and the few passengers using platform 2 had to cross the lines on the level. The newspaper van is in a siding formed in 1971 by removing the west end of the through line. (J.A.M.Vaughan)

2nd-SINGLE SINGLE-2nd
Fremington to
Fremington   Fremington
Barnstaple Jn.   Barnstaple Jn
BARNSTAPLE JUNCTION
(W)   3d   FARE   3d   (M)
Conditions see over For Conditions see over

← 16. No. 25225 has propelled its train of milk tankers from Torrington into the yard on 6th October 1978. This became the last goods depot in North Devon and handled wagon load traffic until 1987. General goods traffic ceased on 5th March 1970. (D.Mitchell)

17. Following closure of "B" Box in May 1971, a ground frame (visible behind the last wagon) was installed at the end of the loop. The remaining signal box, east of the station, closed in 1987. Here we see no. 31286 hauling ball clay from Marland Works on 22nd March 1982, the last year for the Torrington route. (D.Mitchell)

FREMINGTON

18.   The station opened as a terminus on 1st August 1854 and only one platform was provided initially, this being the one on the right in this view towards Barnstaple. This was still the case in 1869, although a passing loop had been provided by then. (A.F.E.Field)

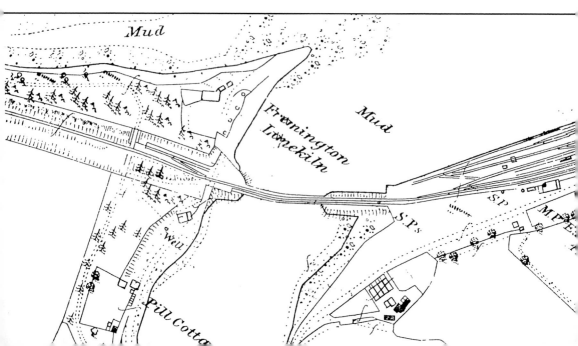

19. A northward view of the down side building on 29th September 1965 includes a Standard 8, one of the millions of post-war motor cars that helped to kill rural railways. (S.J.Taylor)

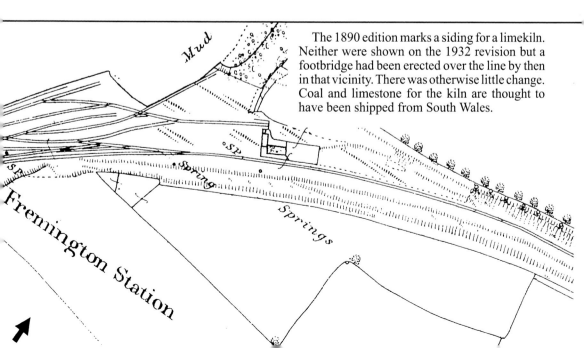

The 1890 edition marks a siding for a limekiln. Neither were shown on the 1932 revision but a footbridge had been erected over the line by then in that vicinity. There was otherwise little change. Coal and limestone for the kiln are thought to have been shipped from South Wales.

20. The signal box was in use until 3rd November 1968 when the loop was taken out of use and two ground frames were provided. Note the masts of a ship and the ladder of the lamp man. (Wessex coll.)

Fremington	1928	1936
No. of passenger tickets issued	3102	1879
No. of season tickets issued	1	10
No. of tickets collected	3026	1836
No. of telegrams	1359	1494
Parcels forwarded	48	45
Parcels received	249	517
Horses forwarded	-	-
Milk forwarded - cans 1928/gallons 1936	-	--
Milk received - cans 1928/gallons 1936	-	-
General goods forwarded (tons)	6752	29
General goods received (tons)	391	178
Coal, Coke etc. received (tons)	144	-
Other minerals forwarded (tons)	12477	3220
Other minerals received (tons)	9665	4751
Trucks livestock forwarded	2	-
Trucks livestock received	2	-
Lavatory pennies	-	56

SOUTHERN RAILWAY.
Issued subject to the Bye-laws, Regulations &
Conditions in the Company's Bills and Notices.

Instow to

Instow to   Instow to
Fremington   Fremington
FREMINGTON

THIRD CLASS   THIRD CLASS
Fare 7½d   Fare 7½d
NOT TRANSFERABLE.

9467

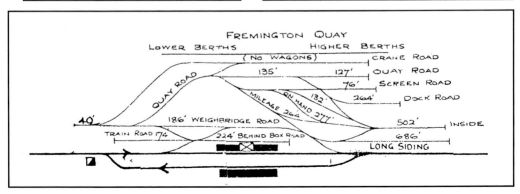

21. The relationship of the quays to the signal box and station building is evident. Coal was the main import, this including locomotive coal for the Exeter district. The peak was 88205 tons in 1942, but even in the 1960s it was not unusual to unload 650 tons of domestic coal in a day. (Wessex coll.)

22. The three Grafton steam cranes of 6-ton capacity were also used for the export of ball clay. After its short rail journey from the pits beyond Torrington, the clay was loaded onto ships for various European destinations. The quay was closed on 31st December 1969, over 14000 tons of clay having been despatched by sea that year. (Wessex coll.)

23.   In the distance is the road crossing to the yard which closed to general goods traffic on 6th September 1965. The 35-ton weighbridge remained in use for weighing wagons loaded with clay until 1979. The object near the camera is the single line key token carrier. (Wessex coll.)

24.   The iron bridge over Fremington Pill replaced the original wooden structure in 1880. The old bridge had a lifting span which enabled small vessels to reach Muddlebridge. A footpath on the bridge was the shortest route between the station and Fremington village. (Wessex coll.)

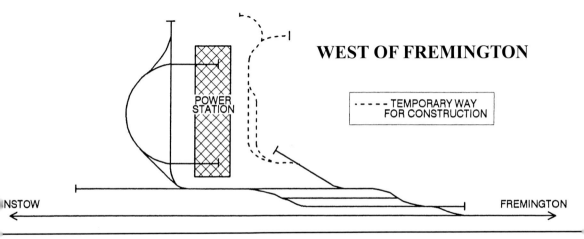

WEST OF FREMINGTON

POWER STATION

```
----- TEMPORARY WAY
      FOR CONSTRUCTION
```

NSTOW ← → FREMINGTON

East Yelland power station was built in 1950-57 and designed to receive all its coal by sea. Railway sidings were provided for the conveyance of construction material and equipment, also coal if necessary. On the rare occasions that coal was unloaded, a crane had to be hired. Once one was brought by rail from Fremington Quay. There was a diesel engine available for shunting until 1974. The power station ceased generating in 1984, the sidings having closed in April 1973.

25.   Generation commenced in 1953 although the station was very incomplete when photographed on 12th April 1952. Originally known as Holloway, the level crossing (lower left) was provided with gates and signals on 25th November 1953. Steam locomotives were used during the construction, these including ex-LSWR class B4 no. 101 and Staverton's 1924 Barclay 0-6-0ST, named *Forth* after the river. (British Electricity Authority)

26.   The waterfront location of the station is well illustrated in this Edwardian postcard view. Beyond the right border of the picture was the 83yd long Instow Tunnel, which was built using the "Cut and cover" method. (Lens of Sutton)

The 1904 survey indicates the substantial marine defences adjacent to the station.

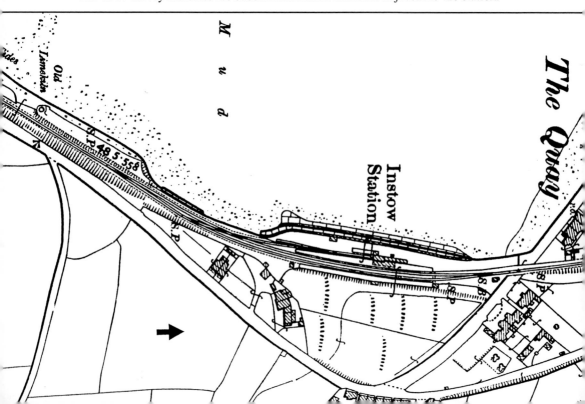

Instow	1928	1936
No. of passenger tickets issued	9041	3280
No. of season tickets issued	71	56
No. of tickets collected	28177	8756
No. of telegrams	525	239
Parcels forwarded	1425	868
Parcels received	3431	8577
Horses forwarded	35	1
Milk forwarded - cans 1928/gallons 1936	-	-
Milk received - cans 1928/gallons 1936	-	-
General goods forwarded (tons)	87	25
General goods received (tons)	297	351
Coal, Coke etc. received (tons)	631	636
Other minerals forwarded (tons)	219	82
Other minerals received (tons)	153	39
Trucks livestock received	-	-
Trucks livestock forwarded	-	5
Lavatory pennies	216	579

27.   The single siding was provided with a gate, a feature normally only found on private sidings. The wide space between the tracks is a legacy of the broad gauge era. The traffic was mostly limited to coal inwards and sugar beet and timber outwards. (Lens of Sutton)

28.   The station opened on 2nd November 1855 and ceased to be staffed on 4th January 1965. A ferry service for foot passengers operated to Appledore on the opposite shore of the River Torridge. Note the extremely unusual profile of the canopy. (A.F.E.Field)

29.   The exterior was recorded in December 1965, two months after the last passenger had left. The building was still standing almost thirty years later and was used by the North Devon Yacht Club. The goods yard had closed on 30th April 1962. (S.J.Taylor)

30.   The view from a clay train on 23rd July 1970 shows that only the up track remained. The loop had been taken out of use on 3rd November 1968 when the box was reduced to controlling the gates and associated signals only. The crossing was equipped with automatic lights on 17th January 1979. (D.J.Aston)

31.   The 1872 signal box survived demolition and became the first such building to be listed by the Department of the Environment (Grade II). The Bideford & Instow Railway Group and Devon County Council have restored it and it is usually open to visitors on first and third Sunday afternoons, Easter to October. Replica crossing gates have been fitted as seen in this 1992 view of a bus enthusiasts' visit. (R.Dark)

32.   In addition to replacing some track and the up starting signal, the BIRG has carefully restored the interior of the box and its 13-lever frame, together with the gate wheel. The population of the village ranged from 600 to 800 during the period of passenger services. (R.Dark)

BIDEFORD GOODS

33.   The goods depot was developed on the site of the broad gauge terminus which was in use from 2nd November 1855 until 10th June 1872, although for standard gauge trains also from 1863. The vessels are an LCT (R) - Landing Craft Tank (Rocket) - and is fitted with 1064 rockets for mass attack of landing beaches. The rocket deck could later be removed and tanks conveyed to the beaches. (R.Dark coll.)

➜   34.   The terminus was in an area known as Cross Parks, remote from the town but convenient for the railway builders. The new station was at the end of the bridge. The goods yard had a crane (left) of 7½ tons capacity and a smaller one in the goods shed. Class M7 no. 23 is shunting on 2nd July 1948. (J.H.Aston)

Bideford	1928	1936
No. of passenger tickets issued	60117	33212
No. of season tickets issued	77	273
No. of tickets collected	106762	92018
No. of telegrams	3019	4018
Parcels forwarded	10978	9278
Parcels received	46605	61126
Horses forwarded	274	52
Milk forwarded - cans 1928/gallons 1936	-	-
Milk received - cans 1928/gallons 1936	-	1834
General goods forwarded (tons)	6467	4554
General goods received (tons)	16856	23178
Coal, Coke etc. received (tons)	8017	7251
Other minerals forwarded (tons)	3597	2077
Other minerals received (tons)	18497	21393
Trucks livestock forwarded	232	444
Trucks livestock received	52	39
Lavatory pennies	2496	1747

➜   35.   General merchandise of all types was handled here but coal arrived by sea rather than rail in the LSWR era. The SR soon closed the wharf and most coal was then brought by train from Fremington. In the 1950s, there were four delivery lorries operating from the depot. The yard closed on 6th September 1965. (Wessex coll.)

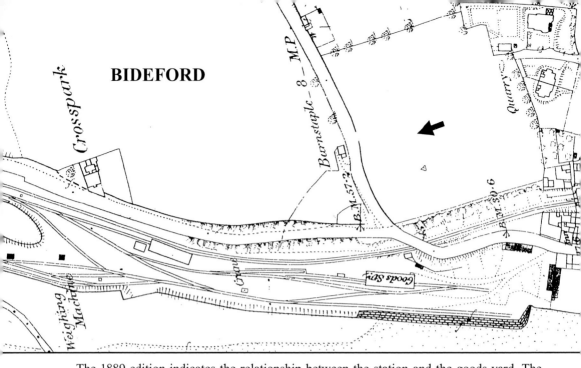

BIDEFORD

The 1889 edition indicates the relationship between the station and the goods yard. The waterfront siding was extended southwards in 1893 to form a private siding for the Western Counties Agricultural Co-operative Society. Large quantities of fertiliser were handled here in conjunction with the Devon Trading Co.

36.   The new station opened on 10th June 1872 and it was used as a terminus for the first three weeks. It was built in a district known as East-the-Water, the main building (illustrated) being on the down side. The brick hard-standing for the horses could still be seen in 1994. (BIRG coll.)

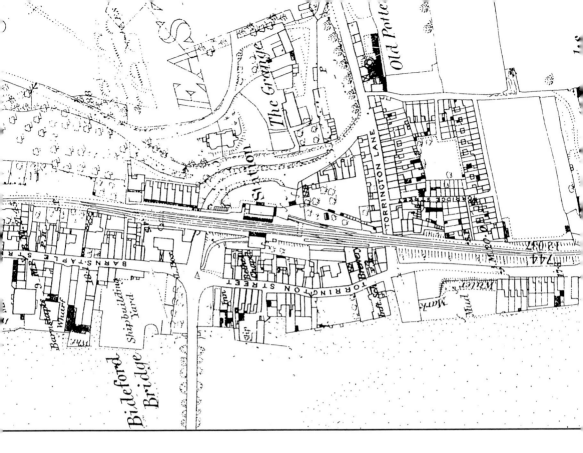

37.   A postcard shows the proximity of the station and Royal Hotel to the bridge to Bideford. Across the river was the station of the Bideford, Westward Ho! & Appledore Railway, which reached Westward Ho! in 1901, Appledore in 1908 and which closed in 1917. (Lens of Sutton)

38.   The Royal Hotel had an entrance from the up platform and also had steps up to a refreshment room. In the distance, a van stands on the short up siding, which was removed in 1959. (D.Cullum coll.)

39.   Evident in this southward view are four canopies of differing styles, the girders of the bridge over the road and the points to the down siding. The population increased from 5742 in 1861 to 10498 in 1961, roughly doubling in the life of the line. (A.F.E.Field)

40.   Heavy flat bottom rail was laid through the station in about 1961. Class 2 2-6-2T no.41314 crosses the public footpath at the north end of the station as it arrives from Barnstaple Junction. (C.L.Caddy coll.)

← 41. The same train was recorded a few minutes later, prior to departure for Torrington. On the right is the 33yd long dock siding which was taken out of use in 1967. Such sidings were once used for loading the horse drawn carriages of the gentry. The signal box had 12 levers. (C.L.Caddy coll.)

0295

SOUTHERN RAILWAY.
This Ticket is issued subject to the By-laws Regulations & Conditions stated in the Company's Time Tables Bills & Notices
Available on day of issue only
BIDEFORD to
CARDIFF
Via Ilfracombe & Campbells Steamer
Bideford   Bideford
Cardiff   Cardiff
3rd CLASS   3rd CLASS
Fare 7/6   Fare 7/6

0295

← 42. The Royal Hotel maintained its elegance while passenger services were in terminal decline. The refreshment room sign had long gone. The up line was taken out of use on 26th February 1967. The station reopened briefly in 1968 when Bideford Bridge was damaged by floodwater. (Lens of Sutton)

43.   The "Exmoor Belle" special train ran to Meeth on 3rd October 1970 and is standing at the roofless weed covered platform. The RCTS/LCGB tour started at Exeter and also visited Ilfracombe. It was the last day of services to that town. (S.C.Nash)

44.　　　Another special ran to Meeth on 9th August 1981 under the name of the "North Devon Explorer". The train was run by Joanes Travel of Barnstaple. In this vicinity, the line is on a shelf on the hillside and in close proximity to dwellings. (J.S.Petley)

SOUTH OF BIDEFORD

　　　Known as Bartlett's sidings, they were used for the timber traffic of E.W.D.Bartlett (Devon) Ltd., (later W.Slee) and also Kynoch Ltd., who had an 0-4-0ST for shunting purposes. The sidings were in use from 1915 until 1965. From 1925, Devon County Council used one for unloading road

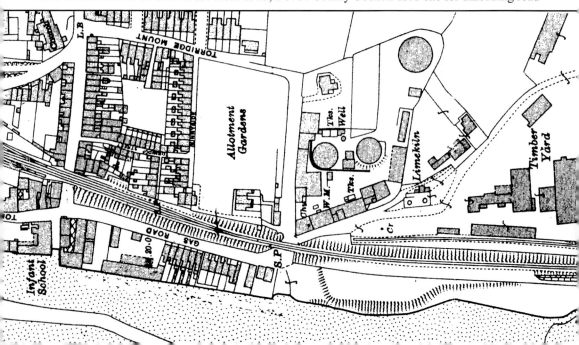

45.   The BIRG have rebuilt the signal box, the original having closed on 26th February 1967 and demolished in 1968. In 1994, it was used as a museum open on Sunday afternoons, Easter to October. Track was relaid, signals replaced and a Mk.I coach was provided for use as a visitors' centre. This 1994 picture does not include the down building which has successively served as a branch of the Midland Bank, a restaurant, an annexe for the Royal Hotel and a centre for the Devon County Council countryside team. (O.Williams)

materials. Other traffic was in connection with the Bideford Gas & Coke Co., Bideford Electric Supply Co., British Petroleum and Shell Mex. The circles represent gas holders on this 1932 edition. The southern part of the line between Bideford and Torrington was built along the route of the Rolle Canal, which was constructed by Lord John Rolle at his own expense. It was in use from 1824 until 1871. The left part of this map overlaps the earlier edition shown above picture no. 37.

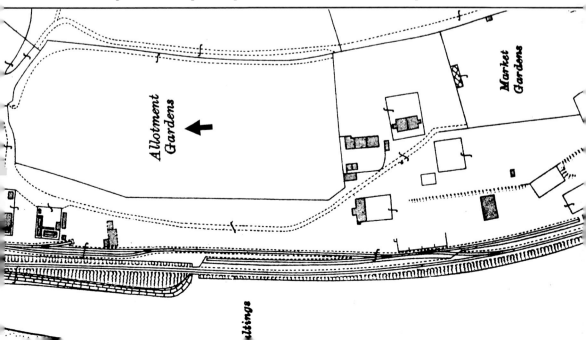

TORRINGTON

46.   The station opened as a terminus on 18th July 1872 and was inconveniently situated, being over 200 ft below the town and one mile distant from it. Centre background is the engine shed and two locomotives, while on the right are two pairs of railwaymen's cottages and the water tank. The cattle dock is in front of the cottages. In the 1930s, a cattle train ran to Chichester twice a month. (Lens of Sutton)

47.   A southward view emphasises that the station was constructed in a hollow in the hillside which restricted future expansion. The road climbs steeply in the background to the town, the population of which declined from 3529 in 1871 to 2920 in 1961. (Lens of Sutton)

The 1904 edition has the line from Bideford and the lengthy headshunt top left. Lower right is the 3ft gauge Torrington and Marland Railway for clay traffic. The two longest of the three sidings radiating from the turntable had served J.B.Reed Ltd since 1883. The company traded in coal and wool, also producing lime in the kiln shown until 1913. The crane (Cr.) was of 5-ton capacity. The road that passes the quarry (lower right) was built on the site of the Rolle Canal, as were the turntable and the tracks north thereof.

S.P

S.P
S.B

Staplevale

Limekiln

Kennels

Engine Shed

Weir

F.B.

Cr.

Rothern Bridge

Torringto
Station

d g e

othern Bridge
Cottage

s Mill
tion

Drummet's
Corn Mill

Quarry

Viaduct

land Y

Torrington	1928	1936
No. of passenger tickets issued	54687	41730
No. of season tickets issued	106	233
No. of tickets collected	59719	47469
No. of telegrams	2853	1481
Parcels forwarded	17297	26664
Parcels received	10614	13879
Horses forwarded	24	27
Milk forwarded - cans 1928/gallons 1936	149	81007
Milk received - cans 1928/gallons 1936	-	13822
General goods forwarded (tons)	2280	2131
General goods received (tons)	3796	3340
Coal, Coke etc. received (tons	6048	6164
Other minerals forwarded (tons)	27657	31483
Other minerals received (tons)	4188	3377
Trucks livestock forwarded	360	270
Trucks livestock received	64	14
Lavatory pennies	456	863

← 48.   Smartly turned out but subjected to swirling steam and rain, class 460 no. 0473 has just arrived with a mixed train from Halwill on 17th June 1926. The locomotive was built for the LSWR by Stephensons in 1884 and was withdrawn in 1928. (H.C.Casserley)

← 49.   The turntable, which was about 48ft long, was removed in the 1920s having been situated in the middle of this view. The line on the left connected to Reed's two private sidings. On the right is the locomotive shed with its inevitable heaps of ash. (A.B.McLeod)

50.   Ex-LBSCR class E1R no. 2696 is taking water on 2nd July 1948, prior to working the 1.15pm freight to Petrockstow. Gloves had once been an important local product despatched in quantity by rail from this station. (J.H.Aston)

51.   Another E1R, no. 32610, was recorded on 20th June 1949, waiting to leave for Halwill at 3.55pm. This was the second and last train of the day and ran at 4.22pm on Saturdays. (S.C.Nash)

52.   Local stone gave a handsome and enduring appearance to the station, which was photographed on 5th August 1955. The coach carries the roof board of the "Atlantic Coast Express". In 1984, the building became the "Puffing Billy" public house. (D.Cullum)

53.   The Austin 10 of the previous picture has been replaced by an Austin A35. This 1963 view shows that the running-in board doubled as a station nameboard to attract those passing by, although the SR had ceased to exist 15 years earlier. (E.W.Fry)

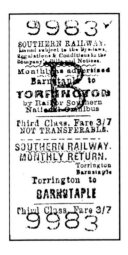
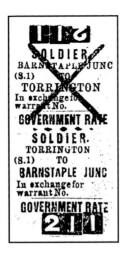
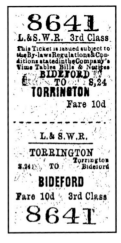

54.   Evidence remained at the south end of the site of the original bridge for the TMR, in which a locomotive was housed overnight. The bridge on the left was for the NDCJLR dated from 1924. The TMR had a loop in the foreground and a single line into the goods yard - see map. (D.Cullum)

55.   Class M7 no. 30250 is shunting the goods shed on 28th September 1956, while main line coaches are berthed in the yard. The lean-to waiting shelter and the crossover between the platforms are distinctive features of this location. (H.C.Casserley)

56.   The water bag seems to be of generous length as class 2 2-6-2T no. 41298 waits to leave for Halwill on 16th August 1958. There had been a staff of 30 here prior to World War II, under a resident station master whose dwelling is largely obscured by the locomotive smoke-box. (A.E.Bennett)

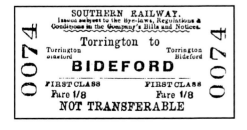

← 57.   The locomotive shed closed on 2nd November 1959 and was photographed on 4th June 1960, shortly before demolition. The three locomotives and ten staff were transferred to Barnstaple Junction. Class 2 no. 41313 is arriving from Barnstaple Junction. (S.C.Nash)

← 58.   The pump house and water tank were on the east side of the station. The up and down water columns are shown in pictures 51 and 56 respectively. Steam power was used to pump water from a well but electricity was used in later years. (Wessex coll.)

59.   General goods facilities were withdrawn on 6th September 1965 but milk tankers continued to pass through the goods shed until the new loading facilities on the up platform were completed in 1975. The shed contained a 2-ton crane. (Wessex coll.)

60.   Taken shortly before the end of scheduled passenger services in 1965, this photograph shows that only three milk tankers could be loaded simultaneously. The sidings on the right were shortened in 1975. (Wessexs coll.)

61.   The unglamorous subject of track maintenance is often neglected so here is the accommodation for the PW trolley, complete with rails over the point rodding. The vehicle was manhandled onto the running lines. (Wessex coll.)

62.   The box had some unusual design features and dated from the opening of the line. It closed on 20th September 1970, two months after it had been photographed. The frame had 30 levers, five of which were spare. (G.Gillham)

63.   The LSWR lower quadrant signal was a rarity when recorded on 22nd July 1970. The down signal in the distance is an SR-style upper quadrant. Class 22 diesel no. D6339 is taking a brake van to Meeth to collect loaded clay wagons. (G.Gillham)

→ 64.   The "Exmoor Belle" is seen on its way to Meeth on 3rd October 1970, by which time the signal arms but not the posts had been removed. Back in 1957, two million gallons of milk had been loaded here for conveyance to London. From 3rd November 1968 until 19th September 1980 single line working was by "staff and ticket". Thereafter it was "one train only". (S.C.Nash)

→ 65.   A new milk loading system, together with an extra roof, was completed in October 1975. The first train was loaded here in March 1976 and the last on 12th October 1978. The fertiliser depot was opened in April 1976 and the last delivery by rail was on 11th January 1980. No. 25225 is proceeding to Meeth with empties, having just deposited loaded fertiliser vans here on 6th October 1978. (D.Mitchell)

66.   The second "North Devon Explorer" pauses on its return from Meeth on 12th September 1982. By that time only a loop remained, together with three truncated sidings. There was a staff of three here from 1965 to 1970 and then only one until 1980. (D.Mitchell)

67.   The last train from Torrington was on 6th November 1982 and was composed of fifteen coaches bound for Bristol behind no. 31158. It is seen from the headshunt. No. 31174 was at the other end of the train which carried 843 passengers. The 1 in 68 down gradient is evident. Track lifting took place in 1984. (D.Mitchell)

Barnstaple Junction to Torrington

	Weekdays												Sundays				
					B			B									
BARNSTAPLE JUNCTION .. d	6 19	7 35	8 45	10 40	13 07	14 50	16 55	..	18 07	20 55	..	11 25	..	16 30	..	18 35
FREMINGTON .. d	6 25	7 41	8 51	10 45	13 12	14 55	17 03	..	18 12	21 00	..	11 30	..	16 35	..	18 40
INSTOW .. d	6 32	7 48	8 58	10 53	13 19	15 03	17 11	..	18 20	21 08	..	11 37	..	16 42	..	18 47
BIDEFORD .. d	6 40	8 02	9 03	10 58	13 25	15 08	17 18	..	18 25	21 13	..	11 44	..	16 50	..	18 54
TORRINGTON .. a	7 00	8 26	9 15	11 10	13 35	15 20	17 28	..	18 37	21 25	..	11 55	..	17 00	..	19 05

Torrington to Barnstaple Junction

	Weekdays												Sundays				
		C	A	B				A									
TORRINGTON .. d	6 58	8 05	8 52	10 05	11 50	13 38	..	15 40	17 45	19 40	..	10 25	..	13 35	..	18 00
BIDEFORD .. d	7 08	8 15	9 05	10 15	12 00	13 50	..	15 50	17 56	19 53	..	10 36	..	13 45	..	18 10
INSTOW .. d	7 15	8 22	9 10	10 22	12 07	13 55	..	15 57	18 02	19 59	..	10 43	..	13 52	..	18 17
FREMINGTON .. d	7 23	8 30	9 20	10 30	12 15	14 03	..	16 05	18 12	20 08	..	10 55	..	14 00	..	18 24
BARNSTAPLE JUNCTION .. a	7 28	8 35	9 25	10 36	12 20	14 08	..	16 10	18 17	20 13	..	11 01	..	14 06	..	18 30

A Through train from Halwill
B Through train to or from Taunton
C Through train to Salisbury

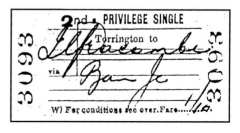

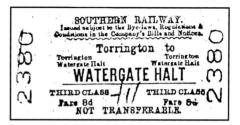

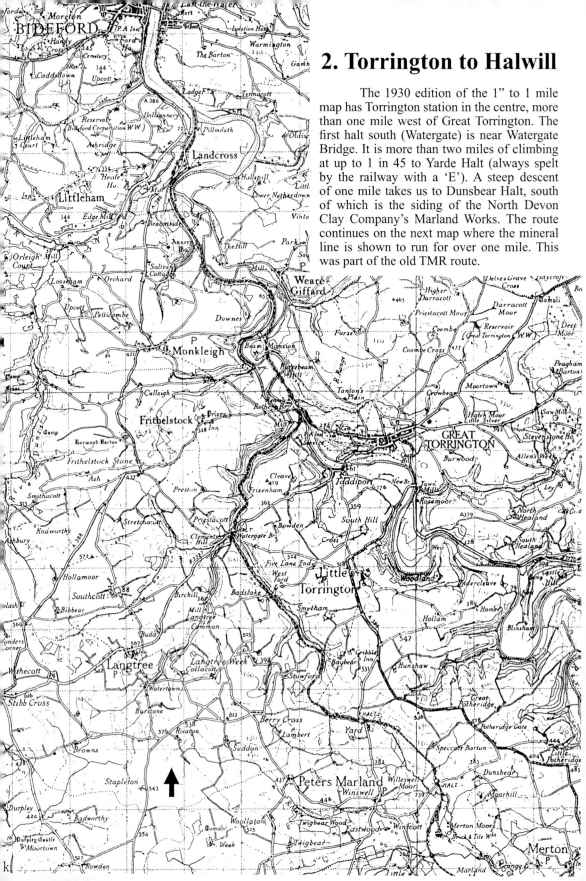

2. Torrington to Halwill

The 1930 edition of the 1" to 1 mile map has Torrington station in the centre, more than one mile west of Great Torrington. The first halt south (Watergate) is near Watergate Bridge. It is more than two miles of climbing at up to 1 in 45 to Yarde Halt (always spelt by the railway with a 'E'). A steep descent of one mile takes us to Dunsbear Halt, south of which is the siding of the North Devon Clay Company's Marland Works. The route continues on the next map where the mineral line is shown to run for over one mile. This was part of the old TMR route.

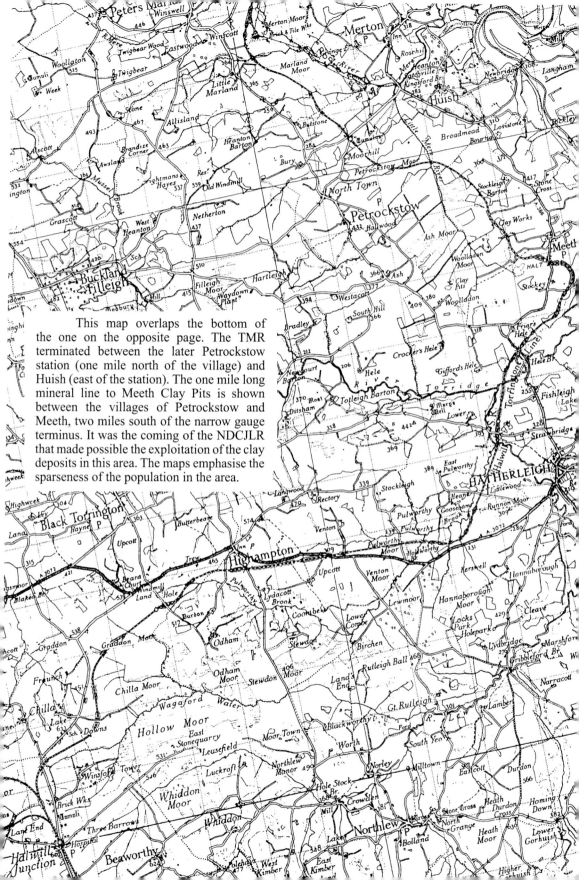

This map overlaps the bottom of the one on the opposite page. The TMR terminated between the later Petrockstow station (one mile north of the village) and Huish (east of the station). The one mile long mineral line to Meeth Clay Pits is shown between the villages of Petrockstow and Meeth, two miles south of the narrow gauge terminus. It was the coming of the NDCJLR that made possible the exploitation of the clay deposits in this area. The maps emphasise the sparseness of the population in the area.

TORRINGTON VIADUCT

68.   A 1912 southward view of the all-timber structure fails to include its full length. Reports suggest that maintenance costs were high. (K.Nunn/LCGB)

69.   The southern end of this fine piece of timber engineering was photographed while 0-6-0ST no. 1 *Mary* returned to Marland Works with empty clay wagons. Torrington station cottages are on the left. (Colonel Stephens Historical Archive)

70.   The TMR wooden viaduct could not be used for the new line on account of its weight limitations and age - 65 years. Stone piers were constructed but one was undermined by flood waters in the winter of 1924. The unconventional Colonel Stephens decided not to demolish it but to winch it upright and underpin it to an annular foundation ring blasted out of the rock of the river bed. (Colonel Stephens Historical Archive).

71.   Class E1R 0-6-2T no. 2124 rumbles over the steel spans as it approaches Torrington from Halwill. Ex-railmotor coaches were in use in the 1930s. The remains of the TMR viaduct are on the left. Inexplicably, the girders had been brought from Halwill by road behind a traction engine instead of by rail to the nearby station. (Dr. I.C.Allen)

WATERGATE HALT

72.   Mixed trains were a common feature on the route south of Torrington and an important means of reducing operating costs. The 10.38am from Halwill is approaching the halt on 28th September 1956, hauled by class 2 2-6-2T no. 41298. (H.C.Casserley)

73.   A few seconds after taking the previous picture, the photographer recorded the short siding which was closed to public traffic on 2nd May 1960. Having been built under a Light Railway Order, the road crossings were ungated. This one is over the B3227. (H.C.Casserley)

74.   The halt opened on 20th September 1926 and is obscured by class 2 no. 41298 working the 10.30am freight from Torrington on 3rd June 1959. Part of the goods yard is on the left and Watergate Bridge is on the right. (J.H.Aston)

DOWN			MONDAYS TO FRIDAYS								SATURDAYS.			
		R		R			P	R	R				To 8th September only	RN
	a.m.	a.m.	"ATLANTIC COAST EXPRESS"	a.m.	"DEVON BELLE"	Mons., Thurs. & Fris. from 21st June	noon	p.m.	p.m.		a.m.	a.m.		a.m.
WATERLOO ... dep.	1A25	9A 0		10A50			12P 0	1A 0	3A 0	...	12A20	1AB25		7A40
Barnstaple Jc. ... arr.	6 41	2 59		3 25			4 43	6 30	8 19	...	5 45	6 41		12 48
Barnstaple Town ,,	7 0	3 7		3 33			4 48	6 38	8 29	...	5 59	7 0		12 56
ILFRACOMBE ,,	7 42	3 46		4 12			5 27	7 17	9 8	...	6 43	7 42		1 39
BIDEFORD ... ,,	7 10	3 28		3 53			5 18	6 58	8 50	...	6 20	7 8		1 15

DOWN						SATURDAYS—continued								
	To 1st September only	R	To 8th September only			30th June to 8th September only		R	"ATLANTIC COAST EXPRESS"	R	"DEVON BELLE"		R	R
		a.m.		a.m.	a.m		a.m		a.m.		noon	p.m.	p.m.	
		8A27		8A34	8A47		10A 5		10A50		12P0	1A 0	3A 0	
WATERLOO ... dep.		1 28		1 45	2 36		2 51		3 45		4 43	6 30	8 19	
Barnstaple Jc. ... arr		1 35		1 55	2 42		2 59		3 54		4 48	6 38	8 29	
Barnstaple Town ,,		2 19		2 40	3 22		3 40		4 36		5 27	7 17	9 8	
ILFRACOMBE ,,				2 16	...		3 28		4 16		5 18	6 58	8 50	
BIDEFORD ... ,,														

DOWN			SUNDAYS			
	R	R	"DEVON BELLE" To 16th September	P	R	
	a.m.	a.m.		noon	p.m.	
	10A50	11AC0		12P0	4A0	
WATERLOO ... dep.	3 27	4 28		4 43	9 46	
Barnstaple Jc. ... arr.	3 37	5 8		4 48	9 53	
Barnstaple Town ,,	4 20	5 49		5 27	10 33	
ILFRACOMBE ,,	3 57	5 8		5 8	10 14	
BIDEFORD ... ,,						

Summer 1951
London through trains

A—Seats may be reserved at a fee of 1/-, upon personal or postal request to the Station Master.   Early application is advisable.   Seats CANNOT be booked by telephone.   B—Depart 1 35 a.m. until 25th August.
C—Depart 11 5 a.m. commencing 1st July   D—Arr. 1 37 p.m. on Mondays, also on Fridays commencing 27th July.   E—23rd June, 15th and 22nd September only.   P—1st and 3rd Class Pullman Cars only between Waterloo and Ilfracombe.   Limited bookings.

RD—Refreshment Car Exeter to Waterloo from 1st July.   R—Refreshment Car between Waterloo and Exeter Central.   RM—Refreshment Car Ilfracombe to Waterloo.   RN—Refreshment Car Waterloo to Ilfracombe.

← 75. Dense woodland surrounded much of the first two miles of the route south of Torrington. Class 2 no. 41308 is hauling the lightly loaded 3.5pm freight from Halwill to Torrington on 4th June 1960. (S.C.Nash)

76. Locally grown larch was the preferred material for pit props in clay mines before open pit working was resorted to in the 1970s. Class 2 no. 41312 is approaching the halt on 25th September 1962. It will have just passed over Vinney Copse crossing. (R.C.Riley)

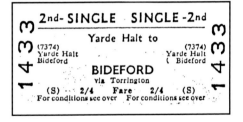

	2nd · SINGLE	SINGLE · 2nd	
6507	(7374) Yarde Halt to	(7374)	6507
	Yarde Halt Dunsbear Halt	Yarde Halt Dunsbear Halt	
	DUNSBEAR HALT		
	(S) 0/6 Fare 0/6 (S)		
	For conditions see over For conditions see over		

	2nd- SINGLE	SINGLE -2nd	
1433	Yarde Halt to		1433
	(7374) Yarde Halt Bideford	(7374) Yarde Halt (Bideford	
	BIDEFORD via Torrington		
	(S) 2/4 Fare 2/4 (S)		
	For conditions see over For conditions see over		

YARDE HALT

77.   This southward view is down the severe 1 in 45 gradient, from the summit, about a half mile behind us. Drivers were required to whistle continuously from the halt to the crossing or for 100 yds in the other direction. The halt opened on 19th July 1926, a surprising afterthought. (N.L.Browne)

78.   A terrace of clayworkers cottages is on the left in this otherwise thinly populated locality. The wagons are vacuum braked and so do not require a brake van. The 3rd June 1959 was a hot day and therefore the exhaust of no. 41295 is not visible. There was no siding here in standard gauge days. (J.H.Aston)

DUNSBEAR HALT

79.   The halt opened with the line and about 70 workers used it each day, many coming from Torrington. This view towards Halwill was recorded in September 1956, the gradient falling here at 1 in 50. (H.Casserley)

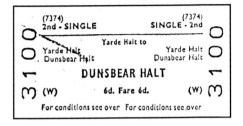

← 80. One of the two waiting shelters is evident on 3rd June 1959 as class 2 2-6-2T no. 41295 runs in with the 1.0pm freight from Torrington, the coach probably running empty to return as the 4.37 from Petrockstow. The loading gauge is over the single siding which closed on 2nd May 1960. (J.H.Aston)

← 81. More shelter was provided here than at the other stopping places, presumably on account of the large number of workers waiting for the afternoon up train. They walked from the works along the trackbed of the TMR, which diverged from the new route here. (J.H.Aston)

82. Smartly painted wooden gates contrast with the grime of no. 41312 on 25th September 1962. In the final year of operation the 06.25 DMU from Torrington terminated here. This was evidently intended for clayworkers but there was no afternoon return train until 19.12. (R.C.Riley)

MARLAND WORKS

83.   This and the next three photographs of 3ft gauge stock were taken on 5th July 1912. No. 1 *Mary* was built by Black, Hawthorn & Co. in 1880 and was in use until 1925. Along with two other locomotives of this wheel arrangement, it was used on the "main line" to Torrington. The wheels were 18 ins in diameter. (K.Nunn/LCGB)

84.   No. 3 *Peter* was produced by Stephen Lewin of Poole in about 1876 and was at Marland from at least 1912 and was scrapped before 1923. There were also seven small diesel engines at various times. (K.Nunn/LCGB)

85.   This is one of three Fletcher Jennings 0-4-0Ts acquired from the Jersey Railway in 1908. Two were rebuilt in 1910 and one was cannibalised but the saddle tanks were carried separately to reduce axle weight. *Jersey I* ran until 1949 and *Jersey II* to 1952; all three were built in the 1870s. (K.Nunn/LCGB)

86.   The TMR carried clayworkers to and from the works in open wagons until two ex-London County Council horse-drawn trams were purchased in 1909 and regauged from 3ft 6ins. They had been in use in the Woolwich area where the tracks were unusual in not being standard gauge. Built in 1882 as double deckers, the stairs were removed but the original longitudinal seat can still be seen on the roof. They were used until 1925, along with three wagons fitted with covers. The public were not carried (officially) but a public freight service (notably for coal) was operated to single sidings at Watergate Yard and Dunsbear. There was also a loop at Yarde, where two four-wagon trains were combined for the descent to Torrington. A locomotive was allocated to each half of the route. (K.Nunn/LCGB)

The Marland Brick & Clay Works Ltd occupied the site from 1879 to 1888, some clay working having been carried out before this period, particularly for the production of material for clay tobacco pipes. The North Devon Clay Co. took over the works eventually and several changes of ownership followed. Ball clay, bricks and roof tiles were produced, although not continuously. The brickworks closed between 1914 and 1923, ceasing production in 1942 for good. Much mining was undertaken between about 1900 and 1969, the internal railway system closing on 6th November 1971. Loading of BR wagons was from road vehicles from 1970 until the siding closed on 12th September 1982.

87.   With the advent of the NDCJLR in 1925, standard gauge shunters became necessary. Five have been in use, two steam and three diesel. This is *Progress*, supplied new by John Fowler & Co. in 1945 and photographed in 1970. The three diesels were purchased by members of the North West Devon Railway Preservation Society for use between Barnstaple and Bideford. As this scheme did not materialise, the locomotives went to the Bodmin & Wenford Railway. (D.J.Aston)

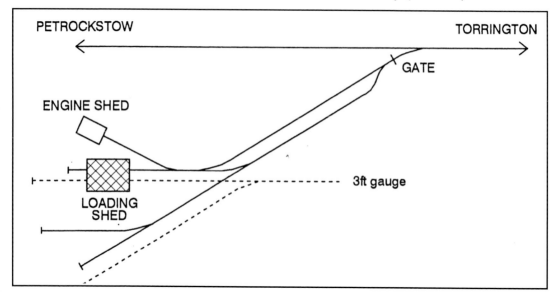

PETROCKSTOW

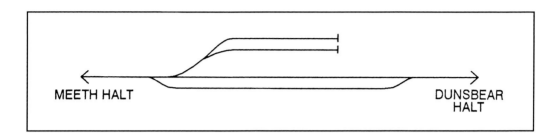

MEETH HALT ← → DUNSBEAR HALT

2nd - SINGLE   SINGLE - 2nd

Hatherleigh to

Hatherleigh   Hatherleigh
Petrockstow   Petrockstow

PETROCKSTOW

(S) 10d.   FARE   10d. (S)

For condit'ns see over   For condit'ns see over

88.   The station was photographed shortly prior to opening and erection of platform nameboards. Colonel Stephens specified buildings of this style on most of his railways but usually they were clad economically with corrugated iron. On the left is the 2 ft gauge temporary way and part of the ground frame on its side. (Lens of Sutton)

89.   The ground frame had seven levers, two of which are visible. Four were for signals and three for points; there were no distant signals. Here we witness the passing of the 10.40am Halwill to Torrington passenger service and the 10.30am Torrington to Halwill freight on 20th June 1949. The locomotive is class E1R no. 32094. (S.C.Nash)

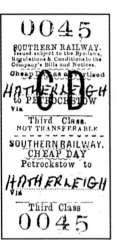

90.   Another E1R was recorded on 16th June 1950 but this had not received the nationalisation prefix of 3 by that date. The coach on the left stood there all day only conveying workmen at each end of the day. The Tyer's electric train tablet apparatus was kept in the booking office. (J.J.Smith)

91.   The same locomotive was pictured on 24th May 1952, by which time it had received its BR number plate. It appears to be adding wagons to an up train. There was a cattle dock (left) but no goods shed or crane. The yard closed on 7th September 1964. (R.S.Carpenter coll.)

92.   The goods yard contained stores for Silcocks animal feed stuffs. Other goods inward included coal and fertiliser, while timber was the main outgoing commodity. No. 41297 is standing with the 4.37pm to Torrington on 9th July 1962, a train that commenced its journey here. (H.C.Casserley)

93.   The village was a mile distant and had a population that diminished from about 400 to 300 during the life of the line. Petrock is recorded as having been a disciple of St. Patrick. Meditating in peace is one of the two men who staffed the station. The guard is about to despatch no. 41312 with the 8.52am Torrington to Halwill on 25th September 1962. (R.C.Riley)

Petrockstow	1928	1936
No. of passenger tickets issued	2692	1417
No. of season tickets issued	7	-
No. of tickets collected	2580	1229
No. of telegrams	-	2
Parcels forwarded	190	315
Parcels received	571	947
Horses forwarded	16	1
Milk forwarded	-	-
Milk received	-	-
General goods forwarded (tons)	253	277
General goods received (tons)	753	994
Coal, Coke etc.	379	384
Other minerals forwarded	63	-
Other minerals received	420	739
Trucks livestock forwarded	154	96
Trucks livestock received	19	16
Lavatory pennies	-	-

← 94. The last through passenger train was recorded on 27th March 1965, the locomotives being class 2 2-6-2Ts nos. 41206 and 41292. Other details of the "Exmoor Ranger" are given in caption no. 12. (S.C.Nash)

← 95. On 26th February 1967, the down loop became a siding, all signals were removed and the final member of staff retired. Class 22 no. D6333 passes through on 22nd July 1970, having climbed the 1 in 50 gradient visible in the background. The station building had been demolished. (G.Gillham)

96. A railman stands on the one remaining siding on 6th October 1978 to see no. 25225 safely across the road. The empty wagons will soon receive another load of ball clay, sometimes incorrectly described as china clay. The clay was once dug as eight inch cubes which soon assumed a ball shape. Much of it is used in the production of sanitary ware and decorative tiles. (D.Mitchell)

SOUTH OF PETROCKSTOW

97.   Lt.Col.Holman F.Stephens was engineer for the construction of the line, the scheme for which had originated back in 1909 as a result of his personal enterprise. It was to be 1922 before work commenced, by which time substantial grants and loans were available from central and local government to improve rural transport and alleviate unemployment. Inexperienced and unsuitable labour caused many problems, notably a drunken riot in Hatherleigh on 23rd June 1923. Stephens' unique career as promoter, engineer and often manager of minor railways throughout Britain has become well known. Other albums in this series to feature his lines include East Kent Light Railway, Branch Line to Selsey, Branch Line to Shrewsbury, Branch Line to Tenterden and Branch Lines around Portmadoc 1923-46. The Colonel is standing in front of an ex-World War I FWD lorry during the construction of Hele Bridge. (Colonel Stephens Historical Archive)

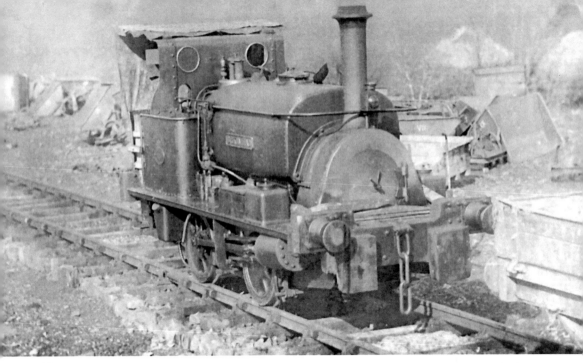

98. A mechanical excavator or "steam navvy" made light work of the heavy clay in this vicinity. Such machines had been used on most new railway works in this century. (Colonel Stephens Historical Archive)

99. The contractors for the construction of the line were P & W Anderson Ltd who used this Hudswell Clarke 0-4-0ST to haul wagons of the type seen in the previous photograph. It was built in 1903 (works no. 650) and later became no. 186 *Birkenhead*. The contractors went into receivership in February 1925 and Colonel Stephens took over the construction work in July, using some of the other six steam locomotives allocated to the contract and hiring direct labour. (Colonel Stephens Historical Archive)

100. The siding for Meeth Works consisted of a loop off the west side of the main line for loading ball clay. Following closure of the line south to Halwill in 1965, buffers were built on the line which was once part of a remarkable man's railway empire. Track lifting was completed in May 1966. No. 31424 is seen with the 09.40 departure on 17th June 1981. The siding closed in August 1982. (S.J.Taylor)

MEETH HALT

101.   The halt and single siding opened with the line, only the loading gauge and the points of the latter being visible in this 1955 northward view. Goods facilities were withdrawn on 7th September 1964. Passenger traffic was slight, as there were usually only two trains per day. (D.Cullum)

102.   The driver of no. 41312 will be sounding his hooter when he restarts his train and crosses the A386 at the regulation 5mph on 25th September 1962. The train is on a 1 in 50 up gradient and will soon be on an eleven chain radius curve, a tough combination. (R.C.Riley)

HATHERLEIGH

103.   This postcard view towards Torrington shows that, as at Petrockstow, the building and sidings were on the up side, but unlike that station access to the sidings was in the opposite direction. The building is now a private dwelling. (Lens of Sutton)

104.   Although the original plan was altered to take the railway nearer to the town, the station was still inconveniently sited, more than one mile from its centre. This was the greatest centre of population on the route, with 1200 residents when the line opened. This dropped to under 1000 upon closure - most travelled by bus, if not car. (Lens of Sutton)

105.   The seven-lever ground frame is on the right. Two wires ran to the lower quadrant signals in the distance and one rod to the nearby point. There was an up fixed distant signal. The booking office housed the single line instrument. (D.Cullum coll.)

106.   Class E1R no. 32610 blows off prior to leaving with the 3.55pm Torrington to Halwill on 20th June 1949. It will pass over three ungated crossings - Pulworthy, Venton and Rosemans Bower. (S.C.Nash)

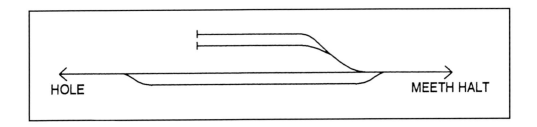

107. The loop could accommodate 21 wagons and a locomotive. Being the principal station on the new route, it had a stationmaster who was also responsible for the adjacent stations. This peaceful scene was recorded on 16th June 1950. (J.Smith)

108.   This and the previous picture include cattle wagons, a reminder of the hectic times when an additional locomotive was required to work extra trains for cattle or sheep between here and Halwill in the early 1950s. There would be up to 50 wagons loaded per week. This 1956 southward view reveals that the original signals had been replaced with posts built from old running rails and upper quadrant arms, a standard SR design. (R.M.Casserley)

109.   Taken on 22nd July 1964, this photograph includes both sidings and both water columns, the only ones on the NDCJLR. Water was pumped up from the River Lew, which joined the River Torridge nearby. Also shown is Bibby's store for animal feeds. (R.Palmer)

Hatherleigh	1928	1936
No. of passenger tickets issued	1706	565
No. of season tickets issued	-	-
No. of tickets collected	2027	684
No. of telegrams	-	28
Parcels forwarded	670	491
Parcels received	2379	3191
Horses forwarded	9	-
Milk forwarded - cans 1928/gallons 1936	-	-
Milk received - cans 1928/gallons 1936	-	-
General goods forwarded (tons)	991	498
General goods received (tons)	1503	1125
Coal, Coke etc. received (tons)	837	904
Other minerals forwarded (tons)	9783	12258
Other minerals received (tons)	1656	941
Trucks livestock forwarded	88	70
Trucks livestock received	4	4
Lavatory pennies	-	-

HOLE

110.   The layout here was almost identical to that at Petrockstow, the cattle dock being visible on the left and the seven-lever ground frame near the centre. There was almost no habitation nearby. (D.Cullum coll.)

111.   The 10.40am from Halwill was captured on film on 20th June 1949, at a time when the SR's bold numbers on the carriage doors left no doubt about the class of travel. Class E1R no. 32610 had been rebuilt in 1929 and was withdrawn in March 1956. (S.C.Nash)

112. Hole refers to a small group of houses, whereas Black Torrington is a village of a few hundred folk, albeit over a mile to the north. To use its name could have caused some confusion with Torrington. Cattle wagons are in store in 1956, most livestock traffic having been lost as the result of the 1955 strike. (R.K.Kirkland)

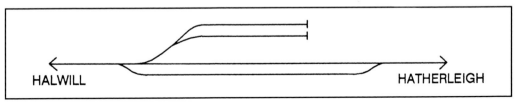

HALWILL   HATHERLEIGH

Hole	1928	1936
No. of passenger tickets issued	1340	329
No. of season tickets issued	-	-
No. of tickets collected	1364	428
No. of telegrams	14	-
Parcels forwarded	227	506
Parcels received	757	1076
Horses forwarded	-	14
Milk forwarded - cans 1928/gallons 1936	-	29
Milk received - cans 1928/gallons 1936	-	-
HGeneral goods forwarded (tons)	505	292
General goods received (tons)	638	980
Coal, Coke etc. received (tons)	292	376
Other minerals forwarded (tons)	-	-
Other minerals received (tons)	1042	1145
Trucks livestock forwarded	7	26
Trucks livestock received	3	2
Lavatory pennies	-	-

113.   Cattle wagons are on the right of this September 1956 view in the Halwill direction. Goods facilities were withdrawn on 7th September 1964. The line was level through the station but climbed continuously to Halwill. (H.C.Casserley)

114.   The 10.38am from Halwill probably only carried the photographer on 22nd July 1964, only weeks before dieselisation and months before total closure. The building was still standing in 1994, although derelict, in this remote wilderness, now a nature reserve. (R.Palmer)

HALWILL

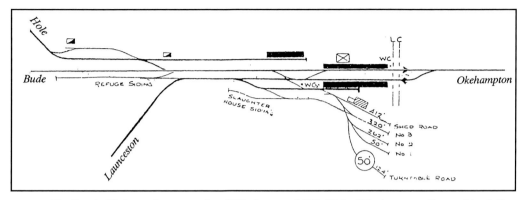

The line to Holsworthy opened on 20th January 1879, Halwill being a small wayside station on it. It became "Halwill Junction" soon after the route south to Launceston came into use on 21st July 1886. The suffix was dropped on 1st January 1923. The diagram shows the track layout from 1925 to 1965.

115. A separate bay platform and run-round loop was added for Torrington trains in 1925. Class E1R no. 2096 is probably leaving the former to shunt at the latter. The mixed train includes an ex-railmotor coach. (D.Cullum coll.)

116.   A further bay platform was provided on the right, this being used mainly for Bude connections although most down trains carried a through portion to that resort. Class 2 no. 41308 is waiting to leave at 6.30pm with a single Bulleid coach for Torrington. (S.C.Nash)

117. With identity obliterated, no. 41313 has a clear signal to leave at 3.0pm for Petrockstow on 12th May 1961. The starting signal was worked from the signal box on the up platform and not the ground frame. The Launceston line is diverging in the foreground. (S.C.Nash)

118. Obscured by the leading van in the previous picture was this ground frame, one of two provided for the loop in 1925. This one also controlled the connection to the main line which was used on a few occasions by the "Atlantic Coast Express". It was sometimes diverted via Torrington, owing to snowdrift blockage in the Okehampton area. (Wessex coll.)

119.   Viewed from the Torrington bay on 24th July 1964 is the slaughterhouse, one of several erected by the LSWR in the West Country. After control by the Ministry of Food in World War I, it passed to local management and provided an important regular traffic to London and the Midlands, via Templecombe. No. 41283 heads the 10.30am departure for Torrington. (J.H.Aston)

Other photographs of this rural junction appear in our *Branch Line to Bude*.

120.   Two groups of meat containers and the water tank appear in this photograph from 25th September 1962. Locomotives arriving from Bude with coaches for attachment to a London train had first to run round them and then draw them back towards Bude. Here we see some waiting to be propelled onto a Waterloo train, while no. 41312 rests in the Torrington bay. The site of this once busy junction is now occupied by a peaceful housing estate. (R.C.Riley)

96